FUN with SECRET CODES
Activity Book

Illustrated by Michael Denman

Warner Press Kids
educate • nurture • inspire

305800210481

When Jesus was 12 years old, Mary and Joseph took Him to Jerusalem.
They were going to celebrate something important.
What was it?

Write the first letter of each picture in the boxes to find out.

God told Noah to build an ark.
When it was finished, he took his family and the animals inside to live.
Why did God want Noah to do this?

Write the letter on the line that comes AFTER the letter under the line.
Then read the answer.

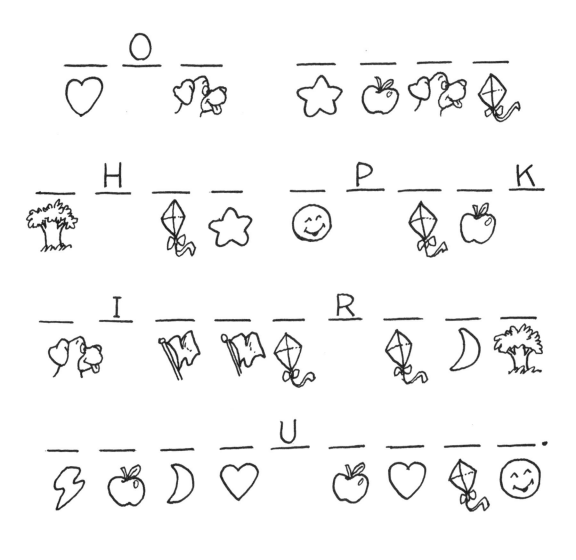

God's people were building a very tall tower.
When God saw it, He was not happy.
What did God do to stop the building?

Use the code to fill in the blanks.
Then read the answer.

___ ___ ___ ___ ___ ___ ___
12 2   4   6   8 10 10

___ ___ ___ ___
 1   3   5   7

___   ___ ___ ___ .
 3   9   2 11

Special visitors brought Abraham a message from God.
Sarah was listening. She laughed when she heard God's message.
What was it?

Use the code on the clock to write the letters on the lines.
Then read the answer.

C N X N T

A
V M S S N A D

A
G D K D C ?

ABCDEFGHIJKLMNOPQRST
UVWXYZ

A crippled man had come to the Pool of Bethesda for 38 years.
Jesus saw him and asked him a strange question.
What was it?

Write the letter on the line that comes **AFTER** the letter under the line.
Then read the answer.

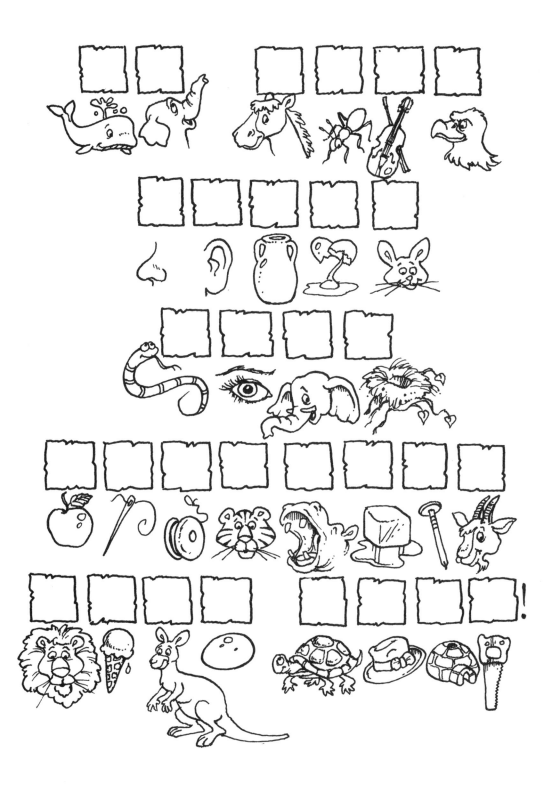

When four men brought their friend to Jesus, Jesus healed him.
The man got up, took his mat, and went home.
The people were amazed!
What did they say?

Write the first letter of each picture in the boxes to find out.

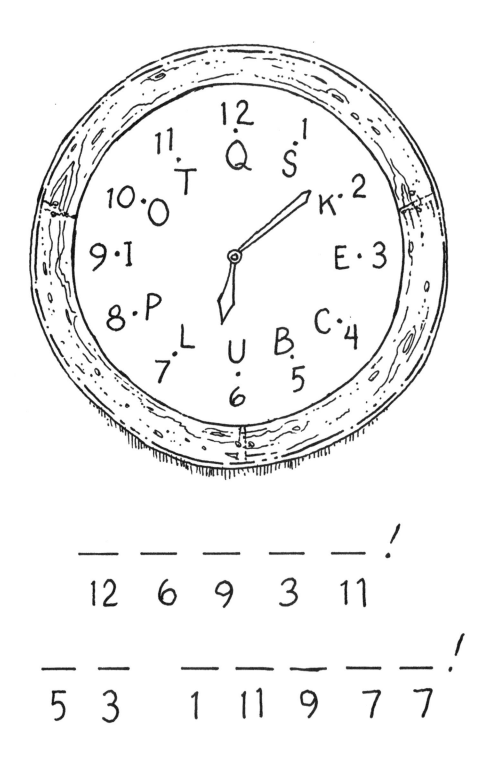

_ _ _ _ _ !
12 6 9 3 11

_ _ _ _ _ _ _ !
5 3 1 11 9 7 7

While Jesus was sleeping on a boat, a terrible storm came.
The disciples woke Him up. "Don't You care if we drown?" they asked.
Then Jesus spoke to the wind and waves.
What did He say?

Use the code on the clock to write the letters on the lines.
Then read the answer.

HE SGD RNM

RDSR XNT

EQDD' XNT

VHKK AD

EQDD HMCDDC.

ABCDEFGHIJKLMNOPQR
STUVWXYZ

Jesus does not want us to be trapped by sin.
He came to set us free!
What does the Bible say about freedom?

Write the letter that comes **AFTER** the letter under the line.
Then read the answer.

The crowds of people following Jesus were hungry.
"Where will we buy bread to feed all these people?" Jesus asked.
Then Andrew brought a boy to Jesus.
What did the boy have?

Use the code to fill in the blanks.
Then read the answer.

$\overline{M}$ $\overline{F}$ $\overline{U}$ $\overline{U}$ $\overline{I}$ $\overline{F}$

$\overline{M}$ $\overline{J}$ $\overline{U}$ $\overline{U}$ $\overline{M}$ $\overline{F}$

$\overline{D}$ $\overline{I}$ $\overline{J}$ $\overline{M}$ $\overline{E}$ $\overline{S}$ $\overline{F}$ $\overline{O}$

$\overline{D}$ $\overline{P}$ $\overline{N}$ $\overline{F}$

$\overline{U}$ $\overline{P}$ $\overline{N}$ $\overline{F}$.

Mark 10:14

ABCDEFGHIJKLMNOPQRST
UVWXYZ

People brought their children to see Jesus.
The disciples thought He was too busy to talk to children.
What did Jesus say?

Write the letter that comes BEFORE the letter under the line.
Then read the answer.

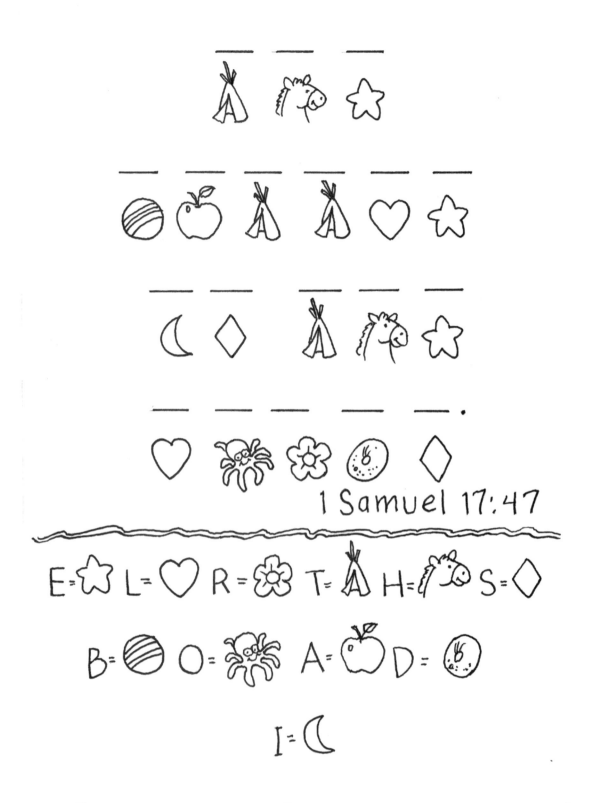

1 Samuel 17:47

When David slung a stone at Goliath, the giant fell down dead!
When we don't feel very strong, what do we need to remember?

Use the code to fill in the blanks.
Then read the answer.

Elijah told the prophets of Baal, "Let's find out who the real God is.
You build an altar to Baal, and I will build one to God.
Then we will call out to them."
How would they know who was God?

Use the code to fill in the blanks.
Then read the answer.

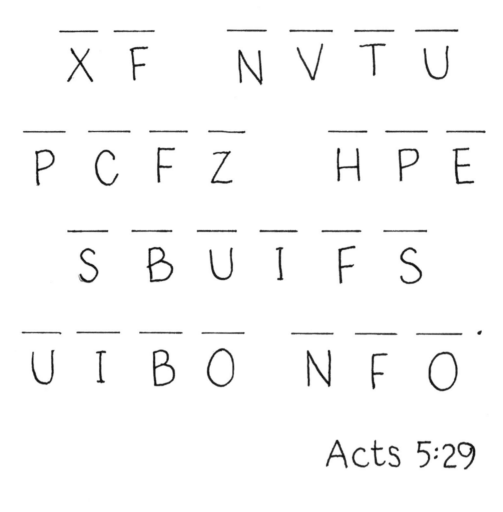

__ __   __ __ __ __
X F   N V T U

__ __ __ __   __ __ __
P C F Z   H P E

__ __ __ __ __ __
S B U I F S

__ __ __ __   __ __ __ .
U I B O   N F O

Acts 5:29

A B C D E F G H I J K L M N O P Q R S T
U V W X Y Z

Bad men put Peter and the disciples in jail for talking about Jesus.
As soon as they got out, they went back to the temple
to teach people again. The bad men were so surprised!
What did Peter tell them?

Write the letter that comes BEFORE the letter under the line.
Then read the answer.

_ H _ _

_ O V _ _

_ O _ .

"Everyone must worship my idol," said the king,
"or they will be thrown into the fiery furnace."
But three men named Shadrach, Meshach, and Abednego did not bow down.
Why?

Use the code to fill in the blanks.
Then read the answer.

$\overline{10}$ $\overline{5}$ $\overline{8}$ $\overline{1}$ $\overline{6}$ $\overline{7}$ $\overline{7}$

$\overline{9}$ $\overline{4}$ $\overline{3}$ $\overline{2}$ $\overline{12}$ $\overline{4}$.

NUMBER CODE:
E=4 L=7 A=2 U=8 W=1 B=9
S=3 F=12 Y=10 O=5 I=6

Paul was on a ship in the middle of the worst storm he had ever seen!
The sailors were afraid they would die.
But Paul told them, "Don't be afraid!
An angel gave me a message in my dream."
What was the message?

Use the number code to fill in the blanks.
Then read the answer.